Saint John's in Pictures

Inquiries should be made to:	Photographs copyright © 1994 Michael Crouser.
THE VERONICA PRESS	Introduction copyright © 1994 Jon Hassler.
Attn: Michael Crouser	
1624 Harmon Place #224	All rights reserved.
Minneapolis, MN 55403	No part of this book may be reproduced or utilized in any form
	or by any means, electronic or mechanical including photocopying,
Library of Congress Catalog	recording or by any information storage and retrieval system,
Card Number: 94-60315	without permission in writing from Michael Crouser.

Saint John's in Pictures

Photographs by Michael Crouser

Introduction by Jon Hassler

The Veronica Press

This book is dedicated to my friend Fr. Angelo Zankl, O.S.B. (SJU '21) who took his first picture at Saint John's 68 years before I took mine.

Here is a book, dear reader, in which you'll find nothing to read. No captions, no headings, no titles. That's because photographer Michael Crouser (SJU '85), has conceived the work as something he calls "an adaptable memoir." The pictures, he says, "don't so much *tell* stories, as *evoke* them. They don't relate memories, they conjure them up."

This collection of Michael's wonderful photos is designed, you see, for a rather exclusive group of people – alumni and others already familiar with Saint John's. It's his hope, he tells me, "that in looking through the book, people might remember and relate some of their own stories and memories – either to someone who doesn't yet know Saint John's, or maybe to an old dorm pal, or just as well to themselves. I've taken the pictures," he says, "but they're everyone's memories. Saint John's is everyone's place, and hopefully there is a picture for everyone."

For me there are dozens. I see Father Angelo in the monastery garden and I think of the unique constancy of a university attached to an abbey. When I returned to Saint John's as a teacher in 1980, for example, I was reunited with the same men who'd been *my* teachers 25 years earlier.

The bricks and mortar, too, speak of constancy. Several shots of the Quadrangle could have been taken last week or a hundred years ago. There's a good bit of my life contained in these pictures. I see the hallway where Father Alfred and I exchanged Middle-English lines of Chaucer on our way to class one fine autumn day in 1954. It's the same hallway where I fell into conversation with Father Alfred in 1981, a day or so after he delivered an All-Souls' homily on purgatory. I told him I hadn't heard purgatory referred to in church for fifteen years, and he replied, "I wanted to demythologize the demythologizers."

And there's the classroom where I failed, despite the longsuffering efforts of Father Dunstan, to learn conversational Spanish. It's the same room where, thirty-five years later, J. F. Powers (one of the most quotable people I've ever known) came to visit my students and talk about writing. He read to them from an Ann Landers column — a marriage problem — and insisted that it was the raw material of fiction. "This is cotton growing in the fields," he said. "Take it and make a shirt."

I see the refectory where I ate approximately two thousand meals as a student and where I still drop in for the occasional lunch or dinner. I'll never forget those four years of cold fried potatoes. I recall one lunch in particular. My aging parents were visiting campus that day, and we sat with Steve Humphrey, who was then coming to the end of his legendary career in the classroom. Lunch turned into an hour-long dialogue, which, if it had a title, would have been called, "Being Young in Minneapolis in the Twenties." They had a wonderful time calling up the details of their youth, right down to the pink lampshades in their favorite ice cream parlor on Hennepin Avenue. When my mother reminded him that there was a telephone on each table and you called in your order, Steve threw his hands in the air and said, with his characteristic mixture of affection, irony and perfect word choice, "Oh, wasn't that smart!" They are dead now, all three of them, but the memory, with the help of these photos, still lives.

But constancy isn't the only quality pervading this plot of ground in central Minnesota. Look at the changes. Look at the young monks in choir, taking the places of the old. Look at the changing faces of the students biking, running, thinking, cheering, graduating. Look at all that cement. I see the photo of the young worshipper in a green shirt and I wonder if he finds it easier than I do to force prayers up through that church ceiling of corrugated concrete. But despite the brooding heaviness of the place, I love dropping in now and then for daily Mass. No hectoring preachers here, no amateur liturgists, no changing the rite from week to week, no dancers performing holy aerobics. Just a low-key, understated Mass, seemingly celebrated by rote and probably the nearest one can get in English to the beautiful meaninglessness of the old Latin liturgy.

One's memories aren't all sublime. I see the sculptured owl in half relief on the west facade of Benet Hall, and I remember living there as a timid freshman, half frightened and half enraged by the six weeks of severe hazing we were put through. I see the classroom desk and I recall the hardness of its seat as I sat through many a painfully tiresome lecture or struggled through an exam I was unprepared for. I see the grave marker in the snow and I think of the friends and relatives and colleagues I've accompanied to the cemetery in the last decade: Father Dunstan. Father Alfred. Betty Powers. Father Constantine. Father Valerian. Just last week, Father Colman. The list goes on.

The primary impression I carry away from these five dozen photos is a reassuring sense of permanence. There's an almost palpable energy growing out of this book that convinces me Saint John's, in existence now for nearly a hundred and fifty years, will continue to thrive for many, many generations to come. I've spent eight years of my life living in Saint John's dormitories, four in the early fifties, four more in the early eighties. During my second residence I recall standing at the window of my room — one of those Marcel Breuer windows with the square eyelids — and watching carloads of visitors hurrying across the campus. It was Homecoming and it was raining. I was struck by how many mothers and fathers were carrying three or four freshly ironed shirts into the dorms for their sons, many of whom, at eleven a.m. were only now getting out of bed, trudging down the hall to the toilet, trudging back, scratching their hair, kicking empty pop cans under their beds. All the students in my building, I realized, were about ten years away from feeling the sentiment of Homecoming. Wait ten years, I thought, and they'll be back with their wives and their little boys and girls. And wait another ten years or so, and they'll be back with their wives and three or four freshly ironed shirts for their sons.

But that's enough of my memories and impressions, dear reader. Turn the pages and find your own.

JON HASSLER (SJU '55)

Special thanks to Pete Crouser (SJU '94) for his invaluable help in producing many of these photographs, to Thomas Riddle for design and typography and Jodi Hills for production assistance. Also thanks to Lee Hanley (SJU '58), Richard Crouser, Thom Woodward (SJU '70), Br. Dietrich Reinhart O.S.B. (SJU '71), Jonathon Kapsner, Otmar Drekonja, John Gagliardi and everyone who made suggestions for, or appears in these pictures.

This book was printed by Diversified Graphics Incorporated in Minneapolis, Minnesota U.S.A.